Walking In Supernatural Faith

Contents

Introduction

When Jesus first saved me, I knew nothing. I did not like to read, and I had trouble studying anything. But by grace, God began to give me a hunger to know Him. He gave me a calling to follow Him and preach the Word. At first, God gave me the *faith* to know Him, to be a believer, that is, a Christian, and to begin to follow Him and to pray. I would go to Him often, and I would cry out in anguish for the things I wanted Him to do. I would fast for days and nights to try to move God. I was fearful, but I had a measure of faith. God brought me trials, and those trials had a purpose.

In time, I received from Him a *supernatural faith.* I stopped crying. I started to abide in Him and in His power. I did not ask for things very much from that point on, because I had great faith that God knew exactly what was best for me. I had learned that if I surrendered myself to Him, He would supply me with more than I could have thought to ask. He would use me to do His will. He would even bless me to do what *I* wanted, knowing my will was submitted to His. He had entrusted me with supernatural faith, and that is what I want to help you to understand and walk in.

The Word of God is a treasure, because it teaches us everything we need to know in order to live and prosper in God. Without the Word, we would not understand faith. I have undertaken to write this brief book about faith, because it is my hope that if we can understand what God says in His Word about faith, we can become part of the 1 percent of Christians who walk, not only by faith, but by *supernatural faith.* By the grace of God, that percentage could increase, and Jesus' Church could begin to manifest true power over the earth.

- *Pastor Armen*

Four Kinds Of Faith

Chapter 1

∞ ∞ ∞

Were you aware that the Bible, the Word of God, teaches about four different aspects or kinds of faith? Most people don't realize the multifaceted nature of faith, and so they do not take advantage of a knowledge that is there for the understanding and for the use of those who will surrender to God.

Part of the problem is that of translation. It is such a blessing that men and women in the past undertook the great challenge of translating the Bible into our common languages. Not only is the Bible translated from Hebrew and Greek into English, but it has been translated into English by dozens of translators. This means that there are dozens of interpretations of the Word, because all translation has to include interpretation. Those translations that attempt to translate each and every Greek and Hebrew word in a word-for-word way, come up against the problem that words in Greek, and especially in Hebrew, often have multiple meanings. Very often, the best English translation (and this goes for any language, not just English) is not what was intended by the original author in the original language.

There are around 3000 Hebrew words. There are around 30,000 English words. Do you see the trouble? In Hebrew, they communicate using fewer words, which means that each word has more possible meanings than each English word. Therein lies the challenge with Bible translation. This is why it is important for some to understand Greek and Hebrew. When it comes to *faith,* this is important to know.

When we go through the whole Bible, we find that there are four kinds of faith. Without getting into the details of the language here, I will list them:

1. Gift of Faith
2. Fruit of Faith
3. Measure of Faith
4. Common Faith

The gift of faith relates to God's power. All faith is supernatural in a sense, because all faith that is true faith is from God. There is such a thing as faith that is not true faith, such as "dead faith." James said "faith without works" is dead faith (Ja 2:26). What he meant was that faith without works is no faith at all. James was not trying to dispute Paul's doctrine of salvation by grace alone. He was saying that we act on what we believe. Taking no action whatsoever, not even the desire to act in obedience to God, is a sign you are not saved.

But of the faith that is not dead, we have these four varieties. The Gift of Faith relates to God's power. The Fruit of Faith deals with your heart and is emotional. You might not have the faith to be physically healed, but you will get emotional comfort from God by faith. This is the fruit of faith.

The Measure of Faith is a natural faith that grows as we exercise godliness. It is what moves you to exercise godliness—to want to grow in Christlikeness. It is a gift from God and you need it.

Common Faith is similar to Measure of Faith in that it is given to all believers and gets you into salvation. It secures your forgiveness and redemption. But it has to be grown. It has to be added to.

Each of these four faiths present something that is available to each and every believer. The Gift of Faith moves for a season, and it leaves again. It is not yours. It is provided for a certain purpose or season. God wants you to do some miracle, to heal someone for example, to prophesy, to pray a powerful prayer. He gives you the faith you need to accomplish His will, even if it is to move a mountain. That is the Gift of Faith.

The Fruit of Faith is Jesus' compassion and emotional healing.

The Measure of Faith and Common Faith are what I am going to refer from here on as Natural Faith (versus Supernatural Faith), and it is up to you to exercise and grow in. It is the beginning point for what I will call *Supernatural Faith.* This book is about moving from the various forms of Natural Faith to Supernatural Faith.

A First Glimpse At Supernatural Faith

Chapter 2

∞ ∞ ∞

In the Bible, we see examples of people with natural faith and people with supernatural faith. Thankfully, we also see examples of people who start out with natural faith and move into supernatural faith. This is encouraging, because almost no one starts out with the kind of supernatural faith that I am aiming to describe in this book.

To contrast the two kinds of faith, consider Nebuchadnezzar, King of Babylon at the time of the Jewish exile, and Daniel, a young Jewish man who had won Nebuchadnezzar's favor as a wise man in his kingdom. You may remember the story as told in the Book of Daniel.

1 In the third year of the reign of Jehoiakim king of Judah came Nebuchadnezzar king of Babylon unto Jerusalem, and besieged it.

2 And the Lord gave Jehoiakim king of Judah into his hand, with part of the vessels of the house of God: which he carried into the land of Shinar to the house of his god; and he brought the vessels into the treasure house of his god.

3 And the king spake unto Ashpenaz the master of his eunuchs, that he should bring certain of the children of Israel, and of the king's seed, and of the princes;

4 Children in whom was no blemish, but well favoured, and skilful in all wisdom, and cunning in knowledge, and understanding science, and such as had ability in them to stand in the king's palace, and whom they might teach the learning and the tongue of the Chaldeans.

5 And the king appointed them a daily provision of the king's meat, and of the wine which he drank: so nourishing them three years, that at the end thereof they might stand before the king.

6 Now among these were of the children of Judah, Daniel, Hananiah, Mishael, and Azariah:

7 Unto whom the prince of the eunuchs gave names: for he gave unto Daniel the name of Belteshazzar; and to Hananiah, of Shadrach; and to Mishael, of Meshach; and to Azariah, of Abednego. (Dan 1:1-7)

God had given Daniel certain natural gifts. He was a man of "no blemish...skillful in all wisdom, and cunning in knowledge, and understanding science..." Daniel was taken into the service of the king along with three of his friends. They were taught the language and were made official "wise men."

But Daniel's natural gifts and abilities paled in comparison to his supernatural gift—his faith. Daniel is someone who from the first time we meet him in scripture has been given supernatural faith. We see the evidence right away. Imagine that you are a young person and your country has been destroyed and scattered by a conqueror who has killed millions of your countrymen, and taken into captivity many others. Now, you have been singled out to be trained and tested as a future councilor to this kingdom. Daniel was to train for three years, in which time, he was to eat the food put before him so that he could continue to grow healthy and strong.

But there was a problem. If Daniel were to eat this food, he would violate his covenant with God. Daniel had no grounds to make demands in his position, but he was determined to obey God, *no matter what*. Look what happened next:

8 But Daniel purposed in his heart that he would not defile himself with the portion of the king's meat, nor with the wine which he drank: therefore he requested of the prince of the eunuchs that he might not defile himself.

9 Now God had brought Daniel into favour and tender love with the prince of the eunuchs.

10 And the prince of the eunuchs said unto Daniel, I fear my lord the king, who hath appointed your meat and your drink: for why should he see your faces worse liking than the children which are of your sort? then shall ye make me endanger my head to the king.

11 Then said Daniel to Melzar, whom the prince of the eunuchs had set over Daniel, Hananiah, Mishael, and Azariah,

12 Prove thy servants, I beseech thee, ten days; and let them give us pulse to eat, and water to drink.

13 Then let our countenances be looked upon before thee, and the countenance of the children that eat of the portion of the king's meat: and as thou seest, deal with thy servants.

14 So he consented to them in this matter, and proved them ten days.
(Dan 1:8-14)

Daniel seemed to have a deeper kind of faith. He seemed to have *supernatural faith*. And God blessed him by giving him favor with the chief eunuch, who was willing to try it Daniel's way, even though he was afraid of the king's displeasure.

This is not the most miraculous thing we see from Daniel in the Bible, but it is the earliest hint that Daniel's faith is a supernatural faith. Look how God then blesses him.

15 And at the end of ten days their countenances appeared fairer and fatter in flesh than all the children which did eat the portion of the king's meat.

16 Thus Melzar took away the portion of their meat, and the wine that they should drink; and gave them pulse.

17 As for these four children, God gave them knowledge and skill in all learning and wisdom: and Daniel had understanding in all visions and dreams.

18 Now at the end of the days that the king had said he should bring them in, then the prince of the eunuchs brought them in before Nebuchadnezzar.

19 And the king communed with them; and among them all was found none like Daniel, Hananiah, Mishael, and Azariah: therefore stood they before the king.

20 And in all matters of wisdom and understanding, that the king enquired of them, he found them ten times better than all the magicians and astrologers that were in all his realm.

21 And Daniel continued even unto the first year of king Cyrus. (Dan 1:15-21)

"God gave them knowledge and skill in all learning and wisdom: and Daniel had understanding in all visions and dreams." The four Jews were found to be the greatest of the bunch, because God had blessed them. Not only did they have supernatural faith, but as they trusted God, He supplied them with an abundance of knowledge, skill, and the supernatural ability to interpret dreams and visions.

When you operate in supernatural faith, you have a massive advantage in life. You are tapped into God's resources. You have only to walk forward in righteousness, obedience, and surrender, and you will see God work through you, blessing your days.

But this all merely sets the scene for what happens next. After we see Daniel's rise as a result of his ability to, not only interpret Nebuchadnezzar's dream, but to know the dream without being told, Daniel's true testing comes.

In contrast to supernatural faith, most people stop short. They have been given the faith for salvation, that is, they have been given what I call *natural faith*. Because Daniel so impressed the king, he decreed that Daniel's God was the true God. In Daniel 2:46-47 it says,

46 Then the king Nebuchadnezzar fell upon his face, and worshipped Daniel, and commanded that they should offer an oblation and sweet odours unto him.

47 The king answered unto Daniel, and said, Of a truth it is, that your God is a God of gods, and a Lord of kings, and a revealer of secrets, seeing thou couldest reveal this secret.

Amazing! The king actually fell prostrate before Daniel. That's how much Daniel was walking in supernatural faith. Nebuchadnezzar then said, "Your God is a God of gods!" This is when Nebuchadnezzar received faith from God by the word of Daniel and a demonstration of the power and presence of God.

Now, we are ready to contrast the faith of these two men. But first, notice that while we have seen all along that Daniel has had supernatural faith from the start, we can also see that

God has tested this faith through trials that have only become progressively harder. If Daniel's faith had failed when he was given the unkosher food to eat, then we would never have heard of him. If he had been afraid to face the king and venture forth his interpretation, he may have been killed along with the other "magicians", and again, we probably would not know who he was. But his next test will be the greatest yet.

Natural Faith Compared To Supernatural Faith

Chapter 3

∞ ∞ ∞

In chapter two, we saw a glimpse of the supernatural faith of Daniel. What makes Daniel's faith so striking is the contrast in the book between his supernatural faith and the merely natural faith of King Nebuchadnezzar. We have already said that the King was won over to a measure of faith by the miracle performed by Daniel. But something happens next which shows an even greater contrast between the king's faith and the supernatural faith of Daniel's three friends, Shadrach, Meshack, and Abednego. Daniel 3 tells us that Nebuchadnezzar made an image of gold and set it up in Babylon. He then made a decree that everyone in the kingdom, whenever they heard a signal, were commanded to fall on their knees and worship the image. The consequence for failing to do so was death by burning in a fiery furnace.

Before we go on, look at this Nebuchadnezzar and the folly of his natural faith. It has already been established that he believed in the one true God, but now he sets up an idol and commands people to worship it. Most scholars believe that the image was of a human form, and most assume that the form was meant to be Nebuchadnezzar's. One feature of natural faith is that it can cause one to be insecure. Nebuchadnezzar believes in God, but he still elevates himself. He not only wants a one-hundred foot statue of himself, but he also insists that other people worship it under penalty of death!

Don't read this and think it only applies to this one guy in history and not to you. After all, you would never set up a one-hundred foot high statue to yourself and expect others to worship it. Or would you? To understand what was in the mind of Nebuchadnezzar, look at someone else who set up a monument to himself, King Saul. The Bible says that he set up a monument to himself around the time that God was rejecting him as king for failing to obey God. Why did he fail to obey God? Because he was afraid of his own people's opinion!

And Saul said unto Samuel, I have sinned: for I have transgressed the commandment of the Lord, and thy words: because I feared the people, and obeyed their voice. (1 Sam 15:24)

How does our merely natural faith cause most of us to set up monuments to ourselves? We don't usually create statues and force people to bow down. We boast. We post on social media some highly curated version of ourselves doing something great so that people will give us "likes". We fish for compliments and the praise of man. We perform for the empty applause of men. This is a version of what both Saul and Nebuchadnezzar were doing. This is a result of only natural faith. To break free of this reliance on the opinions of others, we need supernatural faith.

At the heart of this desire for the praise of man is fear. Our fear of insignificance drives much of our sinful behavior. But a constant feature in the people who have supernatural faith is fearlessness. Now, we can show the contrast between Nebuchadnezzar and Daniel's three friends. Look at Daniel 3. We have already said that Nebuchadnezzar had set up an image and decreed that all people would worship it. Look what happens next. The music plays, and most of the people do as they were commanded, but not Daniel's friends. Some people notice this, and they go to the king.

10 Thou, O king, hast made a decree, that every man that shall hear the sound of the cornet, flute, harp, sackbut, psaltery, and dulcimer, and all kinds of musick, shall fall down and worship the golden image:

11 And whoso falleth not down and worshippeth, that he should be cast into the midst of a burning fiery furnace.

12 There are certain Jews whom thou hast set over the affairs of the province of Babylon, Shadrach, Meshach, and Abednego; these men, O king, have not regarded thee: they serve not thy gods, nor worship the golden image which thou hast set up.

13 Then Nebuchadnezzar in his rage and fury commanded to bring Shadrach, Meshach, and Abednego. Then they brought these men before the king.

14 Nebuchadnezzar spake and said unto them, Is it true, O Shadrach, Meshach, and Abednego, do not ye serve my gods, nor worship the golden image which I have set up?

15 Now if ye be ready that at what time ye hear the sound of the cornet, flute, harp, sackbut, psaltery, and dulcimer, and all kinds of musick, ye fall down and worship the image which I have made; well: but if ye worship not, ye shall be cast the same hour into the midst of a burning fiery furnace; and who is that God that shall deliver you out of my hands?

16 Shadrach, Meshach, and Abednego, answered and said to the king, O Nebuchadnezzar, we are not careful to answer thee in this matter.

17 If it be so, our God whom we serve is able to deliver us from the burning fiery furnace, and he will deliver us out of thine hand, O king.

18 But if not, be it known unto thee, O king, that we will not serve thy gods, nor worship the golden image which thou hast set up.

19 Then was Nebuchadnezzar full of fury, and the form of his visage was changed against Shadrach, Meshach, and Abednego: therefore he spake, and commanded that they should heat the furnace one seven times more than it was wont to be heated.

20 And he commanded the most mighty men that were in his army to bind Shadrach, Meshach, and Abednego, and to cast them into the burning fiery furnace. (Dan 3:10-20)

Do you want to see what supernatural faith looks like? Look again at what Shadrach, Meshach, and Abednego say to the king when he threatens to have them killed in the fiery furnace.

16 Shadrach, Meshach, and Abednego, answered and said to the king, O Nebuchadnezzar, we are not careful to answer thee in this matter.

17 If it be so, our God whom we serve is able to deliver us from the burning fiery furnace, and he will deliver us out of thine hand, O king.

18 But if not, be it known unto thee, O king, that we will not serve thy gods, nor worship the golden image which thou hast set up. (Dan 3:16-18)

"We think God will save us, but even if he doesn't, we won't disobey him." This is incredible. They believe that one of two things is true. God will prevent them from dying in the fire, *or* he has ordained this day for their martyrdom. That is supernatural faith, because it says to God, "Your will be done." Shadrach, Meshach, and Abednego have totally surrendered to God. Nebuchadnezzar with the natural faith is furious. Sometimes those with natural faith are threatened by those with supernatural faith. He orders them burned.

21 Then these men were bound in their coats, their hosen, and their hats, and their other garments, and were cast into the midst of the burning fiery furnace.

22 Therefore because the king's commandment was urgent, and the furnace exceeding hot, the flames of the fire slew those men that took up Shadrach, Meshach, and Abednego.

23 And these three men, Shadrach, Meshach, and Abednego, fell down bound into the midst of the burning fiery furnace.

24 Then Nebuchadnezzar the king was astonished, and rose up in haste, and spake, and said unto his counsellors, Did not we cast three men bound into the midst of the fire? They answered and said unto the king, True, O king.

25 He answered and said, Lo, I see four men loose, walking in the midst of the fire, and they have no hurt; and the form of the fourth is like the Son of God.

26 Then Nebuchadnezzar came near to the mouth of the burning fiery furnace, and spake, and said, Shadrach, Meshach, and Abednego, ye servants of the most high God, come forth, and come hither. Then Shadrach, Meshach, and Abednego, came forth of the midst of the fire.

27 And the princes, governors, and captains, and the king's counsellors, being gathered together, saw these men, upon whose bodies the fire had no power, nor was an hair of their head singed, neither were their coats changed, nor the smell of fire had passed on them. (Dan 2:21-27)

Shadrach, Meshach, and Abednego had entrusted themselves to God. Would they go to be with Him today, or would God prevent their deaths? In this case, it was God's will to save them as a witness to his power and protection. It says in verse 25 that Nebuchadnezzar saw a fourth man in the furnace. This was the angel of the Lord, or perhaps Christ himself, come to protect the young men from the flames. They emerged unburned. Not even their clothing was singed. The result was that Nebuchadnezzar was moved into an even deeper faith than before.

28 Then Nebuchadnezzar spake, and said, Blessed be the God of Shadrach, Meshach, and Abednego, who hath sent his angel, and delivered his servants that trusted in him, and have changed the king's word, and yielded their bodies, that they might not serve nor worship any god, except their own God.

29 Therefore I make a decree, That every people, nation, and language, which speak any thing amiss against the God of Shadrach, Meshach, and Abednego, shall be cut in pieces, and their houses shall be made a dunghill: because there is no other God that can deliver after this sort.

30 Then the king promoted Shadrach, Meshach, and Abednego, in the province of Babylon. (Dan 3:28-30)

Do you think supernatural faith is only for Bible characters? Let's keep reading. By the end of this book I hope to inspire you to walk in the supernatural faith that God has made available to those who will surrender to Him.

More Examples And Contrasts

Chapter 4

∞ ∞ ∞

In chapter three, we saw the contrast between the supernatural faith of Daniel and the natural faith of Nebuchadnezzar. Let's do some more comparing and contrasting, because I want you to see that it's not just one or two people in the Bible who had supernatural faith, but there were many. They were all human. They were all born in sin in a sinful fallen world. They were all in need of God's grace. They needed God to give them faith. Like you and me, they had to learn to trust God, no matter what.

Daniel and the Lions

After Nebuchadnezzar, Persia was ruled by other kings. Daniel continued to have favor in the kingdom. In Daniel 6, we learn that Darius had become king. The king had recognized Daniel's wisdom and power, and he gave him significant influence over the kingdom. Those who were jealous of Daniel tricked the king into making an official decree that no one was allowed to pray to any god except Darius himself for thirty days. Anyone who violated this decree must be thrown into a den of hungry lions. The king agreed, not realizing the extent of Daniel's devotion to God and his supernatural faith. In Daniel 6:10-15 it says,

10 Now when Daniel knew that the writing was signed, he went into his house; and his windows being open in his chamber toward Jerusalem, he kneeled upon his knees three times a day, and prayed, and gave thanks before his God, as he did aforetime.

11 Then these men assembled and found Daniel praying and making supplication before his God.

12 Then they came near, and spake before the king concerning the king's decree; Hast thou not signed a decree, that every man that shall ask a petition of any God or man within thirty days, save of thee, O king, shall be cast into the den of lions? The king answered and said, The thing is true, according to the law of the Medes and Persians, which altereth not.

13 Then answered they and said before the king, That Daniel, which is of the children of the captivity of Judah, regardeth not thee, O king, nor the decree that thou hast signed, but maketh his petition three times a day.

14 Then the king, when he heard these words, was sore displeased with himself, and set his heart on Daniel to deliver him: and he laboured till the going down of the sun to deliver him.

15 Then these men assembled unto the king, and said unto the king, Know, O king, that the law of the Medes and Persians is, That no decree nor statute which the king establisheth may be changed.

The king really liked Daniel. He was "sore displeased with himself" for allowing himself to be tricked into signing the irrevocable decree. We are not told Daniel's emotional state, but it seems clear that God wants us to see that Daniel is unphased by the whole thing. Verse 10 says that as soon as Daniel heard of the decree, he got down on his knees right in front of his window.

Now, you might have had the courage to go on praying to God in secret, but not many people would have done it right in front of the window. This is supernatural faith. Daniel prayed this way every day, and he was not about to stop. At this point, scholars think Daniel must have been about ninety years old. He wasn't going to lose faith now after all these years. He prayed, even though he knew the king's decree. Like Shadrach, Meshach, and Abednego before him, he must have reasoned that God would save him, or that if it was not God's will to save him, then he would be fine with it.

Supernatural faith surrenders to God. Everyone we will look at from Scripture who had supernatural faith has surrendered their life to God. Being a Christian is believing in Jesus' work on the cross to save you. You believe you are a sinner, and you believe that God has sent His Son to die for your sins. It takes what I am calling "natural faith" to do that. But "supernatural faith" leads you further. You don't just trust Jesus for your death, but also for your life. You lay down your life for Him. You die to yourself and live for Him. You surrender to Him and to His plan for you. Daniel is a perfect example of one who had done this.

Interestingly, Darius was not without a strong faith in Daniel's God. Why? Because he knew Daniel. Look at what happens next, and pay close attention to the words of the king.

16 Then the king commanded, and they brought Daniel, and cast him into the den of lions. Now the king spake and said unto Daniel, Thy God whom thou servest continually, he will deliver thee.

17 And a stone was brought, and laid upon the mouth of the den; and the king sealed it with his own signet, and with the signet of his lords; that the purpose might not be changed concerning Daniel.

18 Then the king went to his palace, and passed the night fasting: neither were instruments of musick brought before him: and his sleep went from him.

19 Then the king arose very early in the morning, and went in haste unto the den of lions.

20 And when he came to the den, he cried with a lamentable voice unto Daniel: and the king spake and said to Daniel, O Daniel, servant of the living God, is thy God, whom thou servest continually, able to deliver thee from the lions? (Dan 6:16-20)

The king, bound by his own decree, has Daniel tossed in with the lions. He says, "I know you serve your God continually. He will deliver you." Did the king have supernatural faith? It seems he has at least a measure of faith. For him to say those words, he must have. But then the king shows his fear. In showing his fear, he shows that there is still a lack of supernatural faith in contrast to Daniel, who was cool as a cucumber. In verse 18 it says that the king passed the whole night fasting and in vigil for Daniel's sake.

Now this is interesting. It seems like a perfectly pious thing to do, fasting and staying awake. But this is not something that someone with supernatural faith would do. Natural faith will lead one to cry out to God, to lament and wail in order to convince God to act. Natural faith will misunderstand the will of God and assume that God has a cry-meter that we must cause to go off before He will help us. People with natural faith forget that God has a will, and He is in charge. Daniel had supernatural faith. He knew God was well capable of saving him. He may have known God would do so — he was a prophet, after all,— but it mattered very little. Daniel entrusted himself to the will of God. Let's keep reading.

21 Then said Daniel unto the king, O king, live for ever.

22 My God hath sent his angel, and hath shut the lions' mouths, that they have not hurt me: forasmuch as before him innocency was found in me; and also before thee, O king, have I done no hurt.

23 Then was the king exceedingly glad for him, and commanded that they should take Daniel up out of the den. So Daniel was taken up out of the den, and no manner of hurt was found upon him, because he believed in his God.

24 And the king commanded, and they brought those men which had accused Daniel, and they cast them into the den of lions, them, their children, and their wives; and the lions had the mastery of them, and brake all their bones in pieces or ever they came at the bottom of the den. (Dan 6:21-24)

The king, having rushed first thing in the morning to see what had happened to Daniel, is pleased to find Daniel alive and well. Imagine the scene. There is Daniel sitting there, lounging with lions cuddling up to him and just hanging out. Maybe Daniel was stroking their heads and scratching under their chins. Daniel said, "O king live forever." He told the king that God had sent His angel and shut the lions' mouths. He said that this was because God had found that Daniel was innocent towards God *and* towards the king, who Daniel had done nothing to harm.

This is supernatural faith! Part of having supernatural faith is walking in "innocence" (or *innocency,* as the King James puts it). If you do not walk in innocence before the Lord, then you do not have supernatural faith. People with only natural faith will sometimes cut corners when it comes to doing what is right and just. Not Daniel. When people cut corners of character and morality towards God, it is because their faith has failed. They are fearful and think they cannot trust God. People with supernatural faith are able to be completely honest, totally courageous, and utterly righteous, *no matter what,* because God protects them, and they trust that whatever happens, it is according to the will of the perfect and loving God.

The king was happy. He was glad to throw the men in with the lions who had tricked him. They were devoured, but Daniel was protected. This had a profound effect on Darius.

> *25 Then king Darius wrote unto all people, nations, and languages, that dwell in all the earth; Peace be multiplied unto you.*
>
> *26 I make a decree, That in every dominion of my kingdom men tremble and fear before the God of Daniel: for he is the living God, and stedfast for ever, and his kingdom that which shall not be destroyed, and his dominion shall be even unto the end.*
>
> *27 He delivereth and rescueth, and he worketh signs and wonders in heaven and in earth, who hath delivered Daniel from the power of the lions. (Dan 6:25-27)*

Darius' faith was increased as a result of this demonstration of the kingdom of God. When we walk in supernatural faith, it allows God to work through us to show His power and His kingdom reign. We walk in the newness of life and the "already" of the kingdom of God, come and coming. Those with no faith, or with only natural faith, will often be moved when they see the work of God in the life of a person with supernatural faith. It worked out well for Daniel too! "So this Daniel prospered in the reign of Darius, and in the reign of Cyrus the Persian" (Dan 6:28).

Three New Testament Examples

Let's look at a few more contrasts, this time from the New Testament. John the Baptist was considered a great man. At times, he seemed to display supernatural faith, standing up to both Jews and Romans, preaching a message of repentance to prepare the way of the Messiah, and baptizing people including Christ himself. It says this about him in Matthew 11:7-15:

7 And as they departed, Jesus began to say unto the multitudes concerning John, What went ye out into the wilderness to see? A reed shaken with the wind?

8 But what went ye out for to see? A man clothed in soft raiment? behold, they that wear soft clothing are in kings' houses.

9 But what went ye out for to see? A prophet? yea, I say unto you, and more than a prophet.

10 For this is he, of whom it is written, Behold, I send my messenger before thy face, which shall prepare thy way before thee.

11 Verily I say unto you, Among them that are born of women there hath not risen a greater than John the Baptist: notwithstanding he that is least in the kingdom of heaven is greater than he.

12 And from the days of John the Baptist until now the kingdom of heaven suffereth violence, and the violent take it by force.

13 For all the prophets and the law prophesied until John.

14 And if ye will receive it, this is Elias, which was for to come.

15 He that hath ears to hear, let him hear.

Wow! "There has not risen one greater than John the Baptist" up to that point. But then Jesus says, "but he who is least in the kingdom of heaven is greater than he." John the Baptist did not have what you and I could have. By faith, and by the power of the Holy Spirit, we can have supernatural faith, along with supernatural power in the name of Jesus. Jesus was prompted to say these things about John because of what had happened just before this. In Matthew 11:2-3 it says:

2 Now when John had heard in the prison the works of Christ, he sent two of his disciples, 3 And said unto him, Art thou he that should come, or do we look for another?

John had done what he was called to do, and then he was thrown in prison by Herod for speaking out against him. This seems to have confused him and prompted him to send two messengers to Jesus. John was saying, "Wait a minute, if you are the Messiah, why am I suffering?" See the difference between John and Daniel (and Daniel's friends)? Daniel, Shadrach, Meshack, and Abednego did not cry out to God in confusion saying, "God, we have followed you, why are you letting this happen?" What they said was, "We know God can save us, but even if he doesn't we trust Him." That is supernatural faith. John was suffering in prison, because his faith was natural at this point. Jesus answered him in Matthew 11:4-6.

4 Jesus answered and said unto them, Go and shew John again those things which ye do hear and see:

5 The blind receive their sight, and the lame walk, the lepers are cleansed, and the deaf hear, the dead are raised up, and the poor have the gospel preached to them.

6 And blessed is he, whosoever shall not be offended in me.

He says, "John, you have all the evidence you need to have a supernatural faith...Blessed is he who is not offended because of Me." Jesus implies John is offended because Jesus is not doing what John wants Him to do. Does that happen to you? You think that God is a genie in a bottle, here to do your will, and when it turns out that you are here to do His will, you get "offended?" Does it rob you of the peace and power of supernatural faith? Does it cause you to refuse to surrender?

You and I do not have to be like John the Baptist, because Jesus said that the least in His Kingdom is greater than John. This means that you can walk in supernatural faith. You have the power and the ability. You belong to the kingdom of God, *but you must act on it.*

Barnabas Versus Ananias

In Acts 4 and 5, we see an illustration of the difference between a mighty supernatural faith, and a tragic natural faith. Acts 4:32-37 tells us that there was a high concentration of the early Church who had supernatural faith.

32 And the multitude of them that believed were of one heart and of one soul: neither said any of them that ought of the things which he possessed was his own; but they had all things common.

33 And with great power gave the apostles witness of the resurrection of the Lord Jesus: and great grace was upon them all.

34 Neither was there any among them that lacked: for as many as were possessors of lands or houses sold them, and brought the prices of the things that were sold,

35 And laid them down at the apostles' feet: and distribution was made unto every man according as he had need.

36 And Joses, who by the apostles was surnamed Barnabas, (which is, being interpreted, The son of consolation,) a Levite, and of the country of Cyprus,

37 Having land, sold it, and brought the money, and laid it at the apostles' feet.

Look how they trusted. Look at the signs and wonders performed among them. Look at their generosity and trust in God's provision. We are introduced for the first time to Barnabas, who will be a powerful and courageous missionary with Paul later and will suffer alongside him. Barnabus sold a field he owned and gave the money to the Church for the mission. This is the kind of thing that people with supernatural faith will do. Then look what happens next in Acts 5:1-6

1 But a certain man named Ananias, with Sapphira his wife, sold a possession,

2 And kept back part of the price, his wife also being privy to it, and brought a certain part, and laid it at the apostles' feet.

3 But Peter said, Ananias, why hath Satan filled thine heart to lie to the Holy Ghost, and to keep back part of the price of the land?

4 Whiles it remained, was it not thine own? and after it was sold, was it not in thine own power? why hast thou conceived this thing in thine heart? thou hast not lied unto men, but unto God.

5 And Ananias hearing these words fell down, and gave up the ghost: and great fear came on all them that heard these things.

6 And the young men arose, wound him up, and carried him out, and buried him.

Barnabas was a man of supernatural faith. He was going to prove this again and again throughout the Book of Acts. I can imagine that he was given positive attention for this. His deed is written for all eternity the Word of God! Ananias and Saphira had been a part of the Church. They had a measure of natural faith. When they heard about Barnabas, and saw the attention he was getting, they wanted to do the same, or at least they wanted to *appear* to do the same.

Peter's words to them are instructive. I'll paraphrase verse 4. "Didn't the field belong to you to do whatever you wanted with it? Nobody said you had to sell it. Nobody said you had to give the money to God. When you lie to men you lie to God! Why in the world would you lie to God?"

Busted! Peter was a prophet. The Holy Spirit revealed the truth to him. But the worst part is that Ananias and his wife later in the chapter were killed by God for their deception! This is extreme, because God is so merciful and patient that rarely do we see this kind of instant justice. Ananias and Saphira may not even have had natural faith. They may have had merely dead faith, no faith. If you think God can be lied to, then you have invented a false god. But the contrast is stark. Barnabas had supernatural faith. This couple had the opposite. If you sense any bit of this satanic spirit in your own heart, repent, and surrender to God. God will forgive you if you repent. He will even move you from dead faith to supernatural faith.

Paul and Silas

Just for our encouragement, let us look at one more example of supernatural faith in this chapter. The Apostle Paul started out as Saul the persecutor of Christians. Acts 9 tells us that Paul was going to Damascus to persecute some more Christians after he oversaw the stoning of Stephen in Acts 7. As he traveled, Christ appeared to him and the flash and sound of his glorified presence knocked Saul to the ground. Jesus saved him and called him in dramatic fashion, rendering Saul blind. After sending Ananias (not the same Ananias who died!) to heal Saul's blindness and preach to him the gospel, Saul accepts a commission from Jesus to preach the gospel to the Gentiles, though his commission came with a promise of suffering for Jesus' name (Acts 9:6).

We see throughout the Book of Acts the extent to which Paul and his companions suffered for the sake of the gospel. He describes some of this in his second letter to the Corinthians.

23 Are they ministers of Christ? (I speak as a fool) I am more; in labours more abundant, in stripes above measure, in prisons more frequent, in deaths oft.

24 Of the Jews five times received I forty stripes save one.

25 Thrice was I beaten with rods, once was I stoned, thrice I suffered shipwreck, a night and a day I have been in the deep;

26 In journeyings often, in perils of waters, in perils of robbers, in perils by mine own countrymen, in perils by the heathen, in perils in the city, in perils in the wilderness, in perils in the sea, in perils among false brethren;

27 In weariness and painfulness, in watchings often, in hunger and thirst, in fastings often, in cold and nakedness.

28 Beside those things that are without, that which cometh upon me daily, the care of all the churches.

29 Who is weak, and I am not weak? who is offended, and I burn not?

30 If I must needs glory, I will glory of the things which concern mine infirmities. (2 Cor 11:23-30).

Why did Paul put himself through all that? It was because he had *Supernatural Faith.* He wasn't the only one either. His friends, Silas, Barnabus, Timothy, Titus all suffered with him, among others. When Paul and Silas were in Philippi, they were thrown in jail, because Paul had set free a young woman who was possessed by a fortune telling demon, stirring up the town. In Acts 16:22-24 it says,

22 And the multitude rose up together against them: and the magistrates rent off their clothes, and commanded to beat them.

23 And when they had laid many stripes upon them, they cast them

into prison, charging the jailor to keep them safely:

24 Who, having received such a charge, thrust them into the inner prison, and made their feet fast in the stocks.

How would you have felt if you were in Paul and Silas' situation? You have come all the way following God to preach to these people. You set a young woman free of the demon that oppressed her, and you get a severe beating, thrown in jail, your feet in stocks. They did not know if they would be punished, stoned, or what would happen the next day. What would you have done? Here's what Paul and Silas did.

25 And at midnight Paul and Silas prayed, and sang praises unto God: and the prisoners heard them.

26 And suddenly there was a great earthquake, so that the foundations of the prison were shaken: and immediately all the doors were opened, and every one's bands were loosed.

27 And the keeper of the prison awaking out of his sleep, and seeing the prison doors open, he drew out his sword, and would have killed himself, supposing that the prisoners had been fled. (Acts 16:25-27)

Paul and Silas thought it was a good opportunity to pray and praise God. Why? They had a supernatural faith. It says the prisoners heard them. God used the situation to bring attention to himself through the supernatural faith and surrender of these disciples. Then, God sent an earthquake that did not harm anyone, but caused the doors to fling open! Again, what would you have done? I'm afraid I would have been out of there. But Paul and Silas somehow sensed that God wanted them to stay there, that God had a plan. That is supernatural faith, because that is *surrender*. Paul belonged to God and God manifested His power in his life. Look what happens next.

28 But Paul cried with a loud voice, saying, Do thyself no harm: for we are all here.

29 Then he called for a light, and sprang in, and came trembling, and fell down before Paul and Silas,

30 And brought them out, and said, Sirs, what must I do to be saved?

31 And they said, Believe on the Lord Jesus Christ, and thou shalt be saved, and thy house.

32 And they spake unto him the word of the Lord, and to all that were in his house.

33 And he took them the same hour of the night, and washed their stripes; and was baptized, he and all his, straightway.

34 And when he had brought them into his house, he set meat before them, and rejoiced, believing in God with all his house. (Acts 16:28-34)

What an amazing story. Don't get so used to these Bible stories that you forget they actually happened to real people who are flesh and blood just like you and me. They are sinners saved by grace, just like us. They have been given the same Holy Spirit and the same measure of faith as we have. They started with the same common, natural faith as we did, but leaned in to surrender and cultivated great trust in God. They are ordinary people who grew into supernatural faith.

Paul's attitude about his life was one of total trust in God. Paul lived for ultimate reality and eternity. When he later wrote a letter to these same Philippians, he said this.

20 According to my earnest expectation and my hope, that in nothing I shall be ashamed, but that with all boldness, as always, so now also Christ shall be magnified in my body, whether it be by life, or by death.

21 For to me to live is Christ, and to die is gain. (Phil 1:20-21)

Paul says that whether he lives or dies, Jesus! He lives for Christ. He goes on to say that he would rather die and go be in the presence of Jesus but that he thinks God probably has more use for him first. He simply doesn't care. If he goes on living, he lives with Christ. If he dies, he dies in Christ and gets to see Him face-to-face. That is supernatural faith. I like to think of the Philippian jailer being read this letter and thinking how true it was about Paul, remembering fondly his salvation and baptism.

When you walk in supernatural faith, to live is Christ and to die is gain!

Receiving Faith

Chapter 5

I want to talk to you now about how we get faith in the first place. There is a famous saying that gets quoted a lot. "Preach the gospel everywhere you go, and if necessary use words." This is commonly attributed to Saint Francis of Assissi, though no one knows for sure. The idea is that our lives are the best method of sharing our faith. There is some truth to it, but in actuality, the Bible never says that anyone is saved by "seeing." It says that we are saved by "hearing." Even Jesus, as much of a miracle worker as He was, was primarily a preacher. Paul describes the process in Romans 10.

8 But what saith it? The word is nigh thee, even in thy mouth, and in thy heart: that is, the word of faith, which we preach;

9 That if thou shalt confess with thy mouth the Lord Jesus, and shalt believe in thine heart that God hath raised him from the dead, thou shalt be saved.

10 For with the heart man believeth unto righteousness; and with the mouth confession is made unto salvation.

11 For the scripture saith, Whosoever believeth on him shall not be ashamed.

12 For there is no difference between the Jew and the Greek: for the same Lord over all is rich unto all that call upon him.

13 For whosoever shall call upon the name of the Lord shall be saved.

14 How then shall they call on him in whom they have not believed? and how shall they believe in him of whom they have not heard? and how shall they hear without a preacher?

15 And how shall they preach, except they be sent? as it is written, How beautiful are the feet of them that preach the gospel of peace, and bring glad tidings of good things!

16 But they have not all obeyed the gospel. For Esaias saith, Lord, who hath believed our report?

17 So then faith cometh by hearing, and hearing by the word of God. (Ro 10:8-17 emphasis added)

Faith is received by hearing the Word of God. 2 Timothy 3:15-16 says,

15 And that from a child thou hast known the holy scriptures, which are able to make thee wise unto salvation through faith which is in Christ Jesus. 16 All scripture is given by inspiration of God, and is profitable for doctrine, for reproof, for correction, for instruction in righteousness.

Paul is telling Timothy that the Word makes you "wise for salvation". Timothy has faith because he has "known the holy scriptures." Faith comes by hearing the Word of God. Timothy heard and believed.

1 Peter 1:22-23 says,

> *22 Seeing ye have purified your souls in obeying the truth through the Spirit unto unfeigned love of the brethren, see that ye love one another with a pure heart fervently:*
>
> *23 Being born again, not of corruptible seed, but of incorruptible, by the word of God, which liveth and abideth for ever. (Emphasis added)*

It is the truth that is obeyed, but the truth must first be heard. When the truth is heard, it lodges into the heart and mind and the spirit of the one who hears. The Word abides *forever.* This is the ordinary faith that secures an inheritance in the kingdom of God and a passage to heaven.

James 1:19-21 says,

> *19 Wherefore, my beloved brethren, let every man be swift to hear, slow to speak, slow to wrath:*
>
> *20 For the wrath of man worketh not the righteousness of God.*
>
> *21 Wherefore lay apart all filthiness and superfluity of naughtiness, and receive with meekness the engrafted word, which is able to save your souls. (Emphasis added)*

James says to listen to the Word and receive it, because the Word heard will "save your souls."

Finally, in Acts 17:11, we are told that Paul, Silas, and Timothy left Thessalonica, where many people rejected the Word preached (although some accepted it) and they went to Berea. The Bereans are given high praise, because they loved the truth. When Paul preached, they listened intently, then they investigated the Word. It says,

These were more noble than those in Thessalonica, in that they received the word with all readiness of mind, and searched the scriptures daily, whether those things were so. (Acts 17:11)

Do you have a "readiness of mind" for the Word of God? This is how saving faith comes. Romans 3:9-12 says,

9 What then? are we better than they? No, in no wise: for we have before proved both Jews and Gentiles, that they are all under sin;

10 As it is written, There is none righteous, no, not one:

11 There is none that understandeth, there is none that seeketh after God.

12 They are all gone out of the way, they are together become unprofitable; there is none that doeth good, no, not one.

This describes the human condition since the fall of Adam in Genesis 3. By virtue of our union with Adam (1 Cor 15:22), we are all born under the same curse. "None is righteous." But the saving "Word" is that One came who was righteous, Jesus Christ, Son of God. Romans 3:20-24 says,

20 Therefore by the deeds of the law there shall no flesh be justified in his sight: for by the law is the knowledge of sin.

21 But now the righteousness of God without the law is manifested, being witnessed by the law and the prophets;

22 Even the righteousness of God which is by faith of Jesus Christ unto all and upon all them that believe: for there is no difference:

23 For all have sinned, and come short of the glory of God;

24 Being justified freely by his grace through the redemption that is in Christ Jesus.

Jesus Christ is the righteousness of God manifested in the Word made flesh. He not only gives the message of salvation, He *is* the message. To hear this Word and to receive it by faith is to know this Word in a saving way. This is how common, what I am calling here, "natural" faith is received. For natural faith to blossom into what I am referring to as "supernatural faith" one must take in this Word, the Gospel of Jesus Christ, and cultivate it. This can be done by intention, but it is also largely done by another method. This we will discuss in the next chapter.

Trials, The Food Of Faith

Chapter 6

∞∞∞

In chapter six, we discussed the way we receive faith, by hearing the Word of God. Now, I'd like to talk about how natural faith grows into a powerful supernatural faith. I'll also take time in this chapter to show examples of biblical characters who display natural faith that grows into supernatural faith.

The food of faith is described by James in the first chapter of his letter to the churches. In James 1:2-4 it says,

2 My brethren, count it all joy when ye fall into divers temptations;

3 Knowing this, that the trying of your faith worketh patience.

4 But let patience have her perfect work, that ye may be perfect and entire, wanting nothing.

Now James is speaking to those with faith. His readers have

heard the Word of God and have received it. He has heard that they are facing trials. They may be facing persecutions, famines, and rejection. James tells them, "Good news, this is the food of supernatural faith!"

What? How is that? James says they should consider it "all joy" because these trials will train them. Peter, in 1 Peter 1:7-9 says,

7 That the trial of your faith, being much more precious than of gold that perisheth, though it be tried with fire, might be found unto praise and honour and glory at the appearing of Jesus Christ:

8 Whom having not seen, ye love; in whom, though now ye see him not, yet believing, ye rejoice with joy unspeakable and full of glory:

9 Receiving the end of your faith, even the salvation of your souls.

Again, speaking of hardships, Peter makes the analogy of their faith to gold. Gold may perish in the refiner's fire, but their faith in such a fire will not perish, but become pure, and lead to "the end of your faith, even the salvation of your souls."

This is an easy image to grasp. Your faith, when it is natural, is in need of refinement. It is in need of "food," so God sends food by the way of trial. How you handle the trial will dictate the impact the trial will have on your faith. Will you stand the test in the fire and come out pure gold with supernatural faith?

Why does trial lead to supernatural faith? It is because a feature of those with supernatural faith is the *trust* that accompanies total surrender to God and His will for their life. We have talked about Daniel, Shadrach, Meshach, and Abednego. They are heroic examples of supernatural faith because they had two qualities deriving from their surrender to God:

1. They believed God could save them from anything.
2. They were willing to trust God's plan if He did not want

to save them.

This is the picture of contentment. It reminds me also of Esther, who understood the will of God for her life, and knew that He was calling her to risk her neck to save her people by going to the king uninvited to intercede. She said, "If I perish, I perish!" That is supernatural faith (and she did not perish)!

Abram to Abraham

Abram, who is known by most as Abraham, was a man of Chaldea who had no children. Did you know that Abraham was the first Christian? The Bible says he was a friend of God. Galatians 3:6-9 says,

6 Even as Abraham believed God, and it was accounted to him for righteousness.

7 Know ye therefore that they which are of faith, the same are the children of Abraham.

8 And the scripture, foreseeing that God would justify the heathen through faith, preached before the gospel unto Abraham, saying, In thee shall all nations be blessed.

9 So then they which be of faith are blessed with faithful Abraham.

The Word says that God "accounted" to him for righteousness. It says in verse 8 that God preached the gospel to Abraham. Abraham showed that he believed the promise of God and proved it by obeying God. When he believed and obeyed, God accounted to him the righteousness of Christ, who would *one day* manifest in flesh and die on the cross for Abraham and his children. This is saving faith.

But Abraham's faith at first was natural faith. He was saved, but he had to learn supernatural faith by the school of affliction. The food of his faith was trial. When the first trials came, Abraham could not digest this food. He failed his tests and his faith stagnated. He was still saved, but he had no supernatural faith. People with supernatural faith may feel fear, but they overcome it because their trust in God is greater than their fear. When there was a famine in the land of promise, Abram and Sarai went down to Egypt. This was natural faith. Did God tell him to go to Egypt? No. He was afraid God would not provide. Look what happened.

11 And it came to pass, when he was come near to enter into Egypt, that he said unto Sarai his wife, Behold now, I know that thou art a fair woman to look upon:

12 Therefore it shall come to pass, when the Egyptians shall see thee, that they shall say, This is his wife: and they will kill me, but they will save thee alive.

13 Say, I pray thee, thou art my sister: that it may be well with me for thy sake; and my soul shall live because of thee.

14 And it came to pass, that, when Abram was come into Egypt, the Egyptians beheld the woman that she was very fair.

15 The princes also of Pharaoh saw her, and commended her before Pharaoh: and the woman was taken into Pharaoh's house.

16 And he entreated Abram well for her sake: and he had sheep, and oxen, and he asses, and menservants, and maidservants, and she asses, and camels.

17 And the Lord plagued Pharaoh and his house with great plagues because of Sarai Abram's wife.

18 And Pharaoh called Abram and said, What is this that thou hast done unto me? why didst thou not tell me that she was thy wife?

19 Why saidst thou, She is my sister? so I might have taken her to me to wife: now therefore behold thy wife, take her, and go thy way.

20 And Pharaoh commanded his men concerning him: and they sent him away, and his wife, and all that he had. (Gen 12:11-20)

Rather than trust in God's promise, Abram concocted a scheme out of his own fearfulness. God had promised Sarai (later Sarah) would bear him a son. Why would Abram need to fear being killed by the Egyptians? He didn't trust God. This began when he went to Egypt in the first place. The famine was a test, a trial meant to grow his faith. He failed the test and stayed in natural faith. More tests and trials would need to come for Abram to grow.

Next came the trials of strife with Lot over the land (Gen 13), and then the battle of the armies when Lot was taken captive (Gen 14). In both of those trials, Abram passed and grew as a result, and God renewed His promise to him. But then, he was tested again. God had promised a son through Sarai. Abram and Sarai became impatient for God's promise. Sarai had an idea. "Take my slave girl, Hagar, and have a son with her in my name." Sarai reasoned that since she owned Hagar, the child would be hers. This was a brand new test for Abram. Surprise, surprise, he failed, and the needle was pointed backward to the natural side of faith.

This caused problems and distress. Just because we pass some of the tests of God, doesn't mean we can coast through life from now on. God will not stop shaping you until you look like Christ. His goal for you is godliness, surrender, supernatural faith, and Christlikeness. Now that Abram has gone backwards, look what happens. After changing his name to Abraham and giving him the covenant of circumcision, God allows Abraham to bargain with Him for Sodom, where Lot lives. The place and the people in it were pure evil. This is progress for Abraham. But then, in chapter 20, God throws out another trial. This is profound. Abraham failed this trial in the past, so he gets to face it again.

1 And Abraham journeyed from thence toward the south country, and dwelled between Kadesh and Shur, and sojourned in Gerar.

2 And Abraham said of Sarah his wife, She is my sister: and Abimelech king of Gerar sent, and took Sarah.

3 But God came to Abimelech in a dream by night, and said to him, Behold, thou art but a dead man, for the woman which thou hast taken; for she is a man's wife.

4 But Abimelech had not come near her: and he said, Lord, wilt thou slay also a righteous nation?

5 Said he not unto me, She is my sister? and she, even she herself said, He is my brother: in the integrity of my heart and innocency of my hands have I done this.

6 And God said unto him in a dream, Yea, I know that thou didst this in the integrity of thy heart; for I also withheld thee from sinning against me: therefore suffered I thee not to touch her.

7 Now therefore restore the man his wife; for he is a prophet, and he shall pray for thee, and thou shalt live: and if thou restore her not, know thou that thou shalt surely die, thou, and all that are thine.

8 Therefore Abimelech rose early in the morning, and called all his servants, and told all these things in their ears: and the men were sore afraid.

9 Then Abimelech called Abraham, and said unto him, What hast thou done unto us? and what have I offended thee, that thou hast brought on me and on my kingdom a great sin? thou hast done deeds unto me that ought not to be done.

10 And Abimelech said unto Abraham, What sawest thou, that thou hast done this thing?

11 And Abraham said, Because I thought, Surely the fear of God is not in this place; and they will slay me for my wife's sake. (Gen 20:1-11)

Oh, Abraham! God is merciful and He gives second chances. It is a tremendous blessing when we get a second chance, and we pass the test that we had previously failed. For whatever reason, Abraham now learns that his own faith is not as strong yet as his fear. He is humbled by this situation. Often, we fail the tests of faith. But if we learn from them and it causes humility and godly sorrow, it is not a total loss. Abraham likely learned here that he needed to trust God *even more.*

A man I know of was an opera singer when he became a follower of Jesus. He loved Jesus and surrendered his life to Him while he was away singing opera. In time, God called the man to become a pastor and a church planter. This was a great trial. The man had worked so hard to get into the entry level of the professional singing career, and now, God was calling him to trade the opera stage for the pulpit. He said "yes" to God and seemed to be on his way to a real supernatural faith.

But as soon as he'd said yes and publicly agreed with his denomination to plant a church, he was assaulted by trial on two fronts. First, he began having dreams every night that the Metropolitan Opera had called and invited him to perform. He would wake up so excited that his long dream had come to fruition. But then, as he realized it was a dream, he would feel sad and confused.

The second front of assault came in the form of worldly success. Suddenly, now that he'd committed himself to laying down his opera career, he began getting job offers that were better than anything he'd received before. Sadly, this wore down the man's resolve, and he backed out of his commitment to plant a church, and took a teaching job, planning to reignite his opera career.

That was a failure. That was a move back from supernatural faith to merely natural. But that wasn't the end of the story. One year later, the man, spiritually dry, struggling in a new place, found that his wife was facing some health challenges. The man found himself on his knees. His wife had revealed that she had a lump on her breast. The man was afraid, so he cried out to God, "Please God, if she could be okay, I will plant a church."

The Lord said to him, "If you think I want you to plant a church, then why aren't you doing it?" The man had been rationalizing up to now, saying, "I think I misheard. God didn't really call me." Now, he had to face the reality that indeed, God had called him, and he was being a Jonah. The whale was about to spit him out on the shore.

The man renewed his commitment to God's plan for his life. He surrendered to God and he canceled his singing engagements and upcoming auditions. He planted a church that grew to over 500 people in ten years. But there is another element of the story that bears revealing. The year that he proceeded to plant the church, the same exact trial that took him out the first time came, but this time it came double. The man got twice as many offers from much greater opera companies than before. This went on for two years. Each time was a challenge for the man, but at the end of two years, he was able to say, "Thank you, but no," without any pang of regret. Then the tests stopped. He had passed and grown in faith. God was so good to give him the second chance, because God did not have to do that. He was under no obligation.

This second test for Abraham, unfortunately, ended in another failure. But God was faithful, and He would not give up on Abraham. Abraham, as I said, is humbled by his repeated failures. Perhaps this is why God gives him the ultimate test. If you know the story, you know that finally, Sarah bears Abraham the son of the promise, Isaac. Can you imagine? Abraham waited for God to fulfill his promise for twenty-five years! What were you doing twenty-five years ago? How much water has flowed under the bridge in that time? How different are you now than the person you were twenty-five years ago? How different is your life? Twenty-five years is a long time to wait in the human sense of time. Abraham had waited a long time. God had fulfilled His promise, and then this happened.

1 And it came to pass after these things, that God did tempt Abraham, and said unto him, Abraham: and he said, Behold, here I am.

2 And he said, Take now thy son, thine only son Isaac, whom thou lovest, and get thee into the land of Moriah; and offer him there for a burnt offering upon one of the mountains which I will tell thee of.

3 And Abraham rose up early in the morning, and saddled his ass, and took two of his young men with him, and Isaac his son, and clave the wood for the burnt offering, and rose up, and went unto the place of which God had told him.

4 Then on the third day Abraham lifted up his eyes, and saw the place afar off.

5 And Abraham said unto his young men, Abide ye here with the ass; and I and the lad will go yonder and worship, and come again to you.

6 And Abraham took the wood of the burnt offering, and laid it upon Isaac his son; and he took the fire in his hand, and a knife; and they went both of them together.

7 And Isaac spake unto Abraham his father, and said, My father: and he said, Here am I, my son. And he said, Behold the fire and the wood: but where is the lamb for a burnt offering?

8 And Abraham said, My son, God will provide himself a lamb for a burnt offering: so they went both of them together.

9 And they came to the place which God had told him of; and Abraham built an altar there, and laid the wood in order, and bound Isaac his son, and laid him on the altar upon the wood.

10 And Abraham stretched forth his hand, and took the knife to slay his son. (Gen 22:1-10)

Pretend with me that you've never heard this story, and you don't know how it ends. This is incredible. None of us has been tested like this. Maybe you know the pain and horror of losing a child, but you were not asked to kill him or her. I know this because this was something that only happened twice. Once was God asking himself to sacrifice his only Son, Jesus Christ, and the other is here with Abraham.

What a test! After all these years and failed tests, Abraham finally passes the greatest one. He has come to the place of supernatural faith. He obeys God and gets ready to slay Isaac and then:

11 And the angel of the Lord called unto him out of heaven, and said, Abraham, Abraham: and he said, Here am I.

12 And he said, Lay not thine hand upon the lad, neither do thou any thing unto him: for now I know that thou fearest God, seeing thou hast not withheld thy son, thine only son from me.

13 And Abraham lifted up his eyes, and looked, and behold behind him a ram caught in a thicket by his horns: and Abraham went and took the ram, and offered him up for a burnt offering in the stead of his son.

14 And Abraham called the name of that place Jehovahjireh: as it is said to this day, In the mount of the Lord it shall be seen.

15 And the angel of the Lord called unto Abraham out of heaven the second time,

16 And said, By myself have I sworn, saith the Lord, for because thou hast done this thing, and hast not withheld thy son, thine only son:

> *17 That in blessing I will bless thee, and in multiplying I will multiply thy seed as the stars of the heaven, and as the sand which is upon the sea shore; and thy seed shall possess the gate of his enemies;*
>
> *18 And in thy seed shall all the nations of the earth be blessed; because thou hast obeyed my voice. (Gen 22:11-18)*

Glory to God! Abraham believed God. He trusted God. He had supernatural faith. The author of Hebrews comments on this in the New Testament, talking about Abraham's supernatural faith.

> *17 By faith Abraham, when he was tried, offered up Isaac: and he that had received the promises offered up his only begotten son,*
>
> *18 Of whom it was said, That in Isaac shall thy seed be called:*
>
> *19 Accounting that God was able to raise him up, even from the dead; from whence also he received him in a figure. (Heb 11:17-19 emphasis added)*

Why did Abraham know that God would raise Isaac somehow? Because God had made a promise to him that Isaac's seed would make a nation. Abraham believed God perfectly, and that is the nature of supernatural faith! All of Abraham's trials from the time he was Abram trained him. That's why we should consider it pure joy when we face trials of many kinds (Ja 1:2-4)!

I could show you many more examples of those in the Bible who were trained from faith to faith, until their natural faith gave way to supernatural faith. I could tell you about Peter who, in his natural faith, made big promises to Jesus about dying with Him, and then ran away and denied three times that he even knew Christ. But that same Peter, trained by his trials and now full of the Holy Spirit, preached boldly and suffered persecution, because he was finally walking in supernatural faith.

I could speak of Elijah, who showed a powerful supernatural faith when he took on over four hundred of the Baal prophets at the risk of his own life, then he became afraid and gave up his supernatural faith for a while, complaining to God that he didn't want to live anymore, because life was so hard. But God strengthened him, and he went back to supernatural faith (1 Kg 19)!

Remarkably, the Bible even tells us that Jesus was trained by his trials. Jesus! He was born perfect and never sinned. The author of Hebrews tells us this:

8 Thou hast put all things in subjection under his feet. For in that he put all in subjection under him, he left nothing that is not put under him. But now we see not yet all things put under him.

9 But we see Jesus, who was made a little lower than the angels for the suffering of death, crowned with glory and honour; that he by the grace of God should taste death for every man.

10 For it became him, for whom are all things, and by whom are all things, in bringing many sons unto glory, to make the captain of their salvation perfect through sufferings. (Heb 2:8-10 emphasis added)

This is astonishing. Jesus walked on the earth as a human according to human ways. When He was being baptized in the Jordan River, John objected, saying, "I need to be baptized by you." Jesus said that this needed to be done in order to fulfill all righteousness. He had to live a life of example. And because his people must suffer to be refined and grow into supernatural faith, so did Christ. His sufferings prepared Him for the cross. His sufferings grew His supernatural faith, although He had it all along.

Even when you begin to walk in supernatural faith, God will not stop training you in this life. If He trained Christ, then He will train you and me. The goal for the Christian is supernatural faith. The food of this faith is trial.

Self-Training

There is one more way to grow in supernatural faith that does not include suffering. The only suffering it does include is the suffering of self-discipline. If you want to grow in faith without waiting around for trials, then study and pray the Word of God. The Jews in the Thessalonian church were weak in faith. Paul, Silas, and Timothy went there to preach, and the weak Thessalonians were difficult to pastor. When they left that place, they went to Berea. The Bible speaks highly of the Jews in Berea. It says,

10 And the brethren immediately sent away Paul and Silas by night unto Berea: who coming thither went into the synagogue of the Jews.

11 These were more noble than those in Thessalonica, in that they received the word with all readiness of mind, and searched the scriptures daily, whether those things were so.

12 Therefore many of them believed; also of honourable women which were Greeks, and of men, not a few. (Acts 17:10-12)

The food of faith is trial, but it is also the Word of God. Perhaps it is true that the more you love and study the Word, the less you must suffer. In this life, no one gets out of some suffering, but if there is a way to have less and still grow in supernatural faith, don't you want that?

Be committed to growing in your faith. Have the courage to tell God, "Lord, grow my faith, whatever it takes."

Enemies Of Faith

Chapter 7

In the last chapter I said that learning the Word of God is, along with trial, a means to growing into supernatural faith. Everyone should learn the Word of God. The Christian should not see this as optional. To know God in His divine Word is why we were created. The soul needs to understand. The Scriptures need to be divided rightly. In order to walk with God, you must know His Word.

Worship is very important if you want to please God. There is a way to worship God, and it is found in Scripture. The Word teaches how to pray and praise in the Psalms. It teaches us how to preach and prophesy in the New Testament. It shows us what we need to know about God and following Him.

But there are enemies of faith that keep us from his Word and from believing his Word. I want to talk about them here. There are three main ones: Laziness, Ignorance, and Evil in the Heart.

Laziness

To be lazy is to be invested in the flesh. Most living things do not have the capacity to be lazy. By instinct they work in order to live. They know what to do, and they go about doing it. A single-celled organism wants to live and works nonstop to feed itself and grow and multiply. If the materials and environment allow for it, it does the exactly perfect thing it needs to do according to its purpose to live. A plant is the very same way. It does not decide to skip soaking up the sun's rays for photosynthesis. It greedily takes as much minerals from the soil, water, and sunlight as it needs to not just survive, but to flourish and bear fruit. Animals too! They have been given instincts by God for the sake of growing and multiplying. They will naturally use their God-given abilities and tools (claws, teeth, camouflage) to survive, thrive, and multiply. All living creatures do this—all but one, the sons and daughters of Adam: humans.

Humans are the only creatures that will choose not to thrive. In our sin, there is a laziness in our flesh that has been a threat to our existence since the fall of man in the garden. Laziness was a problem back in Bible times. Look what Solomon said in his Proverbs. "The soul of the sluggard desireth, and hath nothing: but the soul of the diligent shall be made fat" (Pr 13:4).

The lazy man has desires, but does nothing about it. You may desire to have supernatural faith, but you must do something about it. "He becometh poor that dealeth with a slack hand: but the hand of the diligent maketh rich" (Pr 10:4).

The lazy man or woman has a "slack hand." The hands are for doing something. Laziness causes us to do nothing. When we do nothing, we get the result of "nothing." Here is one more: "The desire of the slothful killeth him; for his hands refuse to labour" (Pr 21:25). This is a powerful truth. It is the "desire" of the lazy man that causes him to refuse to labor. You may say that you desire something, but your actions will follow your true desires. Is your true desire to do nothing? Is your true desire to avoid going to any trouble? Is it inertia?

If this is the case, and I believe it is, you and I must *cultivate our desire*. Jesus said to the sleeping disciples who were supposed to be praying, "the spirit indeed is willing, but the flesh is weak" (Mt 26:41). The Spirit desires for us to have supernatural faith, but we must command our flesh to desire the same. We must pray and ask God to help us to stay focused on our true desire to have all that God promises for us, to have supernatural faith and walk in it. We must align our desires with His desires. Then and only then, will our actions follow and laziness turn to diligence.

Ignorance

I wrote some about this in the last chapter, but ignorant is perhaps what you *were* before reading this book. Maybe you truly did not know, were not aware, of the possibility of supernatural faith. Maybe you thought supernatural faith was only for Bible heroes. No, God's desire is that all His people would walk with Him in supernatural faith. It is your destiny, should you choose to take it up. Hosea 4:6 says,

> *My people are destroyed for lack of knowledge: because thou hast rejected knowledge, I will also reject thee, that thou shalt be no priest to me: seeing thou hast forgotten the law of thy God, I will also forget thy children.*

This is a hard word. Lack of knowledge destroys, but look at what else it says. It says that they have "rejected knowledge." It is true that some may not have heard, but for the vast majority today, it is not that the knowledge of the Word of God has not been made known, but that it has been rejected. Ignorance is bliss, we think, and the more we know, the more we are accountable to do. Do not forget "the law of thy God." Go to His Word to remedy your ignorance.

In Scripture this is called being "blind." Having knowledge is having light, truth, illumination, understanding. Set aside time to study the Word of God with the mind to obey what you learn there. Go to a church where the Bible is taught faithfully and you will no longer be ignorant.

I once died in the hospital. At this time, spiritually, I was dumb. I was ignorant. I didn't know anything. I began to study. I studied the Word of God forty hours a week. I did this for ten years. When I died, and Jesus sent me back to my body, I was shaken. I understood that someday I will die, and I needed to learn. I needed to learn so that I could live out the rest of my life with supernatural faith, surrendered to God, not ignorant. And as I learned, I grew.

Evil in the Heart

The third enemy of the faith that I want to deal with here is what the Bible calls "evil in the heart" or "Filthiness." James 1:19-21 says,

19 Wherefore, my beloved brethren, let every man be swift to hear, slow to speak, slow to wrath:

20 For the wrath of man worketh not the righteousness of God.

21 Wherefore lay apart all filthiness and superfluity of naughtiness, and receive with meekness the engrafted word, which is able to save your souls.

We need to be "slow to wrath," because we are called to "worketh the righteousness of God." Working the righteousness of God is walking in supernatural faith. But James says we must "lay apart all filthiness and superfluity of naughtiness." Superfluity means a large amount of something, or more of something than is necessary. In the case of naughtiness and filth, any amount is a "superfluity." James is saying that you cannot work righteousness and walk in supernatural faith unless you lay apart sin. Acting on the evil in your flesh is a perfect way to be sure that you will not walk in supernatural faith.

Eph 4:17-19 shows us how the filthiness of sin and the ignorance of mind go hand in hand.

17 This I say therefore, and testify in the Lord, that ye henceforth walk not as other Gentiles walk, in the vanity of their mind,

18 Having the understanding darkened, being alienated from the life of God through the ignorance that is in them, because of the blindness of their heart:

19 Who being past feeling have given themselves over unto lasciviousness, to work all uncleanness with greediness.

"Gentile" means "the cursed ones." To not walk according to faith is to be cursed. See how Paul is saying that they are in ignorance if they do this? Their hearts are blind, so they have "given themselves over unto lasciviousness, to work all uncleanliness with greediness." We are to "work righteousness," rather than working "uncleanness," which is the opposite. If not, you will not only fail to walk in supernatural faith, but you will stay among the "cursed ones," yourself a cursed one.

These are the enemies of faith, and you must crucify them in your flesh by loving and holding to the Word of God. Your crying does not move God. Only the Word moves God, especially the Word acting in the lives of His children.

Psalm 25:3 says, "Yea, let none that wait on thee be ashamed: let them be ashamed which transgress without cause." Wait on the Lord, and you won't be ashamed. To have supernatural faith is to be surrendered to God, to wait on Him, trusting Him. If you "transgress," that is, you break God's laws, you sin, you necessarily transgress "without cause." The only reason to transgress is that you have no faith. Go to the Word and live.

Psalm 45:7 says, "Thou lovest righteousness, and hatest wickedness: therefore God, thy God, hath anointed thee with the oil of gladness above thy fellows." Do you hate wickedness and love righteousness? This verse is about Jesus. Jesus loved his Father's ways, so He was "anointed with the oil of gladness." It says this about David as well. (we know it was about Jesus, because the author of Hebrews tells us so in Hebrews 1:9.) "Above thy fellows" means that David and Jesus were the gladdest people ever. How do we get glad? By loving righteousness and hating wickedness. Wickedness is an enemy of supernatural faith. Righteousness feeds it.

So flee these enemies of supernatural faith and move toward the oil of gladness that comes from righteousness. Turn your back on laziness, ignorance and evil in the heart and turn toward Jesus and a surrendered life.

Supernatural Faith

Chapter 8

Hebrews 11:1 says, "Now faith is the substance of things hoped for, the evidence of things not seen."

When a person comes to Jesus, God gives them faith, what I've been calling "natural faith." It is the faith that saves, but otherwise you can *choose* to ignore it and walk in flesh. It is legitimate faith. Imagine natural faith as a machine that, if you only knew how to turn it on, would make you a millionaire, but you cannot, because you don't know how. You don't speak the language that the instructions are written in.

God gives you the machine of supernatural faith. He gives you with your natural faith all nine spiritual gifts and all nine spiritual fruits. The gifts He gives are:

Gifts of healing
Gifts of prophecy
Gifts of tongues
Gifts of the interpretation of tongues
Gifts of faith for miracles

Gifts of discerning of spirits
Gifts of preaching
Gifts of apostleship
Gifts of knowledge

There are other gifts in the Bible, but those are the main ones. Additionally, God gives us the nine fruits of the Spirit. They are:

Love
Joy
Peace
Patience
Kindness
Goodness
Gentleness
Faithfulness
Self-control

These gifts and fruits dwell in you by the Holy Spirit when you have been born again. The machine is there. The potential is there. But for it to operate properly, you must walk in supernatural faith. Imagine your natural faith like a container. God gives you this to play with. Even when you don't walk in the totality of supernatural faith, you can access this power. He will let you. He will use you from time to time. This can have a way of growing your faith and leading to supernatural faith *if you let it.* It is not a total victory, only partial. You may not be able to do everything that Jesus did, but by His grace, you can do some of the things. You have all of it, but in your experience, only a small part of it is usable. It is enough to allow you to see some of God's power and be used a little, but it is not enough for the total victory God desires for you. That victory comes by supernatural faith.

Imagine faith is like a container of tissues. You can pull them out one at a time if you are operating in natural faith. But if you walk in supernatural faith, surrendered to God, then you can have the whole thing. Pulling out one tissue at a time might look like someone who is walking along looking in many ways like a typical nonbeliever. He is fearful, he is losing the battle with his sin, but occasionally, he prays for someone and they get healed. Or occasionally, he shares a word from God and someone is blessed. Sadly, many Christians stop there and never progress beyond it.

If you want powerful results in your life, you need supernatural faith. Supernatural faith is something you get dragged into. In the Old Testament, there is no word for faith. The concept is described there as "trust." This makes perfect sense. Supernatural faith is extreme trust. This is why to walk in supernatural faith you must be fully surrendered to God. Fully. Totally. What part of you can you hold back from God? None! No part! It's all His! Accept that, and walk in supernatural faith.

Walking your whole life in natural faith is like being a thief who asks God to help him steal. It's like being a liar who asks God to help her get one over on someone. If you are not submitted to God and His ways totally, you are not trusting Him, you are not surrendered, and you are not going to experience the fruit of supernatural faith.

In Hebrews 11, we see the men and women of supernatural faith from the Old Testament. These were not perfect people, but at some point in their lives, they surrendered to God, and He used them mightily. This is the "confidence in what we hope for, and the assurance about what we do not see." This confidence, this hope and assurance, this supernatural faith changes you completely.

I was a nobody. Like many other preachers just starting out, I was stupid, nothing. Nobody cared about what I thought or was teaching. I hated to read books. There was nothing good in me, but God called me to supernatural faith. When you have supernatural faith, you are important to everybody, because God is important to everybody and now you represent Him. But supernatural faith does come with a price. People love natural faith, because when you stop at natural faith, nothing is asked of you. Now, rich people, poor people, all people call me, because they know I have supernatural faith.

Recently I told God, "I'm going to Dallas." I know my God will use me anywhere. A lady came to me and said, "If you go to Dallas, I'll buy the land." I did not pray for the land. Anywhere you go with that faith, God will be there. You will carry Him there. You will prosper living for God alone. Your existence there will benefit God and He will bless you because of your supernatural faith.

Having God in your life means that supernatural faith is always there. But to have supernatural faith and only walk in natural faith is like going to war with a machine gun, but you don't know how to use it. A man I know was in the Air Force. Except for fighter pilots and a few special forces units, very few members of the Air Force ever experience combat. Ninety-five percent of the men and women of the Air Force are there to support those five percent who fight. This man was not a combat soldier. However, once, he was deployed with his squadron into Haiti when the U.S. was intervening and getting rid of a dictator. No one knew if there would be any resistance from the Haitian military. This man loaded and unloaded cargo planes, but because of the unknown threat, everyone was issued an M-16. Not a "gun guy," the man had no experience with guns except for the two days, two years prior that he'd been trained on the machine gun in basic training. But now, though on paper he was qualified, since he hadn't touched a gun in two years, he could not even remember how to load it or shoot it! This man was lucky that there was no resistance, and he was not called upon to use his weapon. Deadly as it was, the thing was useless to him.

This is exactly what walking in natural faith is like. All the power of the universe lives in you and is at your disposal, but you have no idea how to access it. The way is total surrender. Faith is trust.

If you go into this third dimension of anointing, meaning you surrender to God and walk in supernatural faith, you don't even have to pray anymore. You carry so much authority walking in the name of Jesus. You'll be like Samuel coming to anoint David. When the people saw him coming, they asked, "Do you come in peace?" Why did they ask that? Because Samuel walks with God, he represents God as a prophet and judge of Israel. If God wanted to smite them, He might send His surrendered servant Samuel. They were rightly concerned and took him seriously.

If you have supernatural faith, when you need something, you just ask God. Nehemiah shows us this. The king asks him, "What do you need?" He says, "My people need a wall." The king says, "Done."

When COVID-19 came, I asked God, "God, what should I do?" He said, "If you pray, no one will die in your church." I called some men from the church to come over to my house and pray. They were afraid, "But Pastor, it's COVID-19." I said, "If you say that one more time, I'm coming over to your house!" They came and I hugged them! They were wearing masks, and I said, "Take it off! God says no one is dying!" And no one has died in our church.

You don't even need to ask God to meet your needs when you have supernatural faith, He *is* your needs. Let Him decide how He's going to take care of you. Trust Him. Put His abiding Word in action and let it dwell in you (1 Pt 1:23).

To conclude this short book: Natural faith is something God gives you to play with, to experience Him sometime. But natural faith is just a school. Along with the Word of God and trials, you can be dragged into supernatural faith. The day you give up living for yourself and start trusting God, completely surrendered to Him, you will experience supernatural faith.

Like the heroes of the Old Testament who trusted God, you will be warned when God is up to something. Noah was warned about the flood. Abraham was warned about Sodom. You will have God's voice including you in His plans.

All my years I cried and fasted. Today, I don't fast. If you are close to Jesus you don't need to. I don't fast for finances. I don't fast for my health. I don't need to fast. I trust God with those things. My crying days are over. Whatever God wants is first with me. I don't even tell Him my desires. I just ask Him what He wants. That is supernatural faith, and you can experience it if you trust Him. Satan will have to ask your permission to do anything, because you come in the name of Jesus.

What will you do now? Can you imagine your life with supernatural faith? Have you taken the risk that is no risk at all and surrendered your life to Christ to do what He wants in and through you? Can you imagine a Church on the earth with supernatural faith? This is what God is waiting for, and this is my prayer for you. I pray the blessing of the Lord on your life, that His Word would dwell in you and that you would trust Him and walk in the mighty power of His great name in supernatural faith! Go forth in God's peace and blessing and be the Church! Come Lord Jesus!

About The Author

Pastor Armen Takhmizyan

Pastor Armen Takhmizyan has an annointed healing and evangelism ministry. The Lord has also gifted him with the ability to interpret dreams, just like Daniel did for King Nebuchadnezzar. Pastor Armen has studied biblical scriptures, theology, and deliverance for over 25 years. He currently lives in California, but plans to relocate permanently to Texas, as he expands the ministry.

www.ingramcontent.com/pod-product-compliance
Lightning Source LLC
Chambersburg PA
CBHW061341120726
48001CB00002B/968